Briefly:
Anselm's *Proslogion*
with the Replies of
Gaunilo and Anselm

David Mills Daniel

scm press

The author and publisher acknowledge material reproduced from
Anselm Proslogion with the Replies of Gaunilo and Anselm,
trans. T. Williams, Indianapolis/Cambridge: Hackett Publishing
Company, ISBN 08722056570. Reprinted by permission of
Hackett Publishing Company, Inc. All rights reserved.

British Library Cataloguing in Publication data

A catalogue record for this book is available
from the British Library

0 334 04038 8/978 0 334 04038 5

First published in 2006 by SCM Press
9–17 St Alban's Place,
London N1 0NX

www.scm-canterburypress.co.uk

SCM Press is a division of
SCM-Canterbury Press Ltd

Printed and bound in Great Britain by
Bookmarque, Croydon, Surrey

Contents

Introduction

The SCM *Briefly* series is designed to enable students and general readers to acquire knowledge and understanding of key texts in philosophy, philosophy of religion, theology and ethics. While the series will be especially helpful to those following university and A-level courses in philosophy, ethics and religious studies, it will in fact be of interest to anyone looking for a short guide to the ideas of a particular philosopher or theologian.

Each book in the series takes a piece of work by one philosopher and provides a summary of the original text, which adheres closely to it, and contains direct quotations from it, thus enabling the reader to follow each development in the philosopher's argument(s). Throughout the summary, there are page references to the original philosophical writing, so that the reader has ready access to the primary text. In the Introduction to each book, you will find details of the edition of the philosophical work referred to.

In *Briefly: Anselm's Proslogion with the Replies of Gaunilo and Anselm*, we refer to *Anselm Proslogion with the Replies of Gaunilo and Anselm*, translated by Thomas Williams, 2001, Indianapolis/Cambridge: Hackett Publishing Company, ISBN 0872205657.

Each *Briefly* begins with an Introduction, followed by a

chapter on the Context in which the work was written. Who was this writer? Why was this book written? With some Issues to Consider, and some Suggested Further Reading, this *Briefly* aims to get anyone started in their philosophical investigation. The detailed summary of the philosophical work is followed by a concise chapter-by-chapter overview and an extensive glossary of terms.

Bold type is used in the Detailed Summary and Overview sections to indicate the first occurrence of words and phrases that appear in the Glossary. The Glossary also contains terms used elsewhere in this *Briefly* guide and other terms that readers may encounter in their study of Anselm's *Proslogion*.

Context

Who was Anselm?

Anselm was born in Aosta, in the north of Italy, in 1033. His father, a nobleman and landowner, opposed his desire to enter a monastery, so he left home, and made his way to Normandy. There he joined the Benedictine Abbey of Bec, where Lanfranc was prior. After Lanfranc moved to Caen as abbot, Anselm replaced him as prior, becoming abbot in 1078. During this time, he encouraged study and research at Bec, and also wrote books himself, including the *Monologion* and the *Proslogion*.

Following William, Duke of Normandy's (William I, 1066–87) conquest of England in 1066, the Abbey of Bec held English lands. As a result of visiting these, Anselm came to be well-regarded in England, and in 1093, after the death of Lanfranc, who had become Archbishop of Canterbury in 1070, William's son, William Rufus (William II, 1087–1100) persuaded a reluctant Anselm to succeed him. As William Rufus had taken over the assets of the archdiocese, acceptance involved Anselm in disputes about the rights of the Church with William and his successor, his brother Henry (Henry I, 1100–35). Anselm was forced to make two visits to Rome, to seek papal support, and on the second occasion, after an absence of four years, was only allowed back into the country two years before his death in 1109. He was canonized in 1494.

What is the *Proslogion*?

In the preface to the *Proslogion*, Anselm tells us about his reasons for writing the book. Encouraged by the monks at Bec, he had written another book, containing arguments for God's existence. However, he was not satisfied with it, because it consisted of a 'chaining together of many arguments'. He wanted a 'single argument', which would stand by itself as a proof of God's existence. This would be a more appropriate kind of argument for a God who depended on nothing else, but on whom everything else depended for its existence and well-being. He applied himself to the task with vigour, but, unable to think of such an argument, and fearing that he was wasting his time, he tried to put it from his mind. However, he could not stop thinking about it, and what has come to be known as the ontological argument finally came to him. It has fascinated philosophers and theologians ever since because, unlike the cosmological and design arguments, which start from experience (or interpretations of experience), it is an *a priori* argument, which moves (with remarkable brevity) from the idea of God to his existence. Anselm records that, after he had written this argument down, the Archbishop of Lyons persuaded him to put his name to both of his books. Anselm also gave them new titles. The first, called, 'A pattern for meditation on the rational basis of faith', became the *Monologion*; the second, 'Faith seeking understanding', the *Proslogion*.

But why did Anselm want to prove God's existence and find a rational basis of faith? As a monk, he not only believed in God, but had dedicated his whole life to God's service. He had all the knowledge of God that he required from God's revelation of himself, in particular through the life and work of Jesus, which is recorded in the Bible, and which he accepted in faith. Talk of finding a rational basis of faith suggests doubts about God's revelation and an attempt to buttress faith with rational arguments.

But this would be to misunderstand Anselm's purpose. Medieval theologians did not see revelation and reason as mutually exclusive sources of knowledge about God, with those who accepted God's revelation in faith discarding reason. They believed that human beings are made in God's image, with a God-given intellect that should be used in God's service. Revelation was the important source of knowledge about God, and some things, such as God being three in one, could only be known through revelation. But other things, like God's existence and such attributes as his goodness, could be known through both reason and revelation. And reason had an important role to play in exploring and understanding what God has revealed. Theology is, after all, an intellectual activity. Anselm wanted to use all the means at his disposal to increase and deepen his knowledge of God, and to get as close as he could to God, so that, as thinker, teacher and religious leader, he would be able to serve God better.

That Anselm's purpose was to extend and deepen his knowledge of a God in whom he already believed is shown by the form of the *Proslogion*. It is written as a prayer, with Anselm frequently asking for God's help. As an 'insignificant mortal', he needs God to teach him 'how to seek you, and show yourself to me when I seek'. He longs to understand God's truth, in which his heart already 'believes and loves'. He does not 'seek to understand in order to believe', but believes, 'in order to understand'. For, 'Unless I believe I shall not understand.'

3

When we think about the traditional arguments for the existence of God, we tend to think in terms of philosophical arguments that are intended to be objective proofs of God's existence. Once they understand the argument(s), even sceptics and outright atheists will be persuaded to believe in God. Understanding precedes belief. This is how the arguments for the existence of God have been regarded in the past, and how some still regard them. But this is not how Anselm sees it. For him, belief not only precedes understanding, but is essential to it. Anselm does not seem to have expected his proof to persuade atheists to set aside their disbelief and embrace theism; the argument would not mean much without pre-existing belief in God. But it will help those who already believe in God through faith to achieve a deeper understanding of him. Following the criticisms of Immanuel Kant (who first called this type of argument 'ontological') and David Hume, in particular, this is how the arguments are generally viewed today: not as philosophical heavy artillery, which pound away atheism, but as explorations of God's nature and his relationship to creation and human beings, which will help to clarify thinking about God and may strengthen faith.

The ontological argument is set out in Chapters II–IV of the *Proslogion*. Anselm asks God to help him to understand that he is (as he is believed to be) something than which nothing greater can be thought: a concept that even the fool (of Psalms 14 and 53) understands. But if this concept exists in the understanding, it could also be thought to exist in reality, which would be greater. And, if that than which nothing greater can be thought exists only in the understanding, something greater than it can be thought. But this is impossible. Therefore, something than which a greater cannot be thought exists both in the understanding and in reality.

Anselm then argues that that than which nothing greater can be thought exists so truly that it cannot be thought not to exist, because something that cannot be thought not to exist is greater than something that seems not to exist. If it can be thought not to exist, it is not that than which a greater cannot be thought, which would be a contradiction. Therefore, it exists so truly that it cannot be thought not to exist. This being is God, and to understand that God is that than which nothing greater can be thought is to understand he exists in such a way that he cannot fail to exist, even in thought.

So, by treating existence as an attribute or perfection, which it is better or greater to possess than not, Anselm considers he has proved not only that God exists in reality, but he has necessary existence, because there is a contradiction involved in thinking that that than which nothing greater can be thought does not exist.

Anselm's argument was quickly subjected to detailed criticism by Gaunilo, a monk of the Abbey of Marmoutier. In his *Reply on Behalf of the Fool*, Gaunilo makes the points that it seemed impossible to accept that even a being than which nothing greater can be thought cannot be thought not to exist, as even God can be thought not to exist; and that Anselm's argument could be used to define anything into existence. He uses the example of a supposedly perfect lost island. It might be argued that, as the island exists in the understanding, and existence in reality is better, it must exist in reality. Gaunilo's first point is also made by David Hume in his *Dialogues Concerning Natural Religion* (Part IX). Whatever we conceive as existent, we can also conceive as non-existent, so there is no being whose non-existence implies a contradiction.

In his *Reply to Gaunilo*, Anselm explains more fully what

he meant by the idea of that than which nothing greater can be thought existing necessarily. Such a being has this type of existence because, as he does not consist of parts, he cannot be thought of as beginning to exist. Only things with a 'beginning or end', which consist of parts, or which do not exist always and everywhere as a whole, can be thought of as not existing. However, it seems perfectly possible to have a concept of such a being, but still to think that it does not exist. Anselm also dismisses Gaunilo's perfect island argument, because there was nothing else to which the argument he put forward in the *Proslogion* could apply, except that than which nothing greater can be thought.

Fatally for acceptance of the ontological argument by the Roman Catholic Church, Thomas Aquinas rejected it in his *Summa Theologica* (Question II, Article I). Referring to the argument that, for the reasons given by Anselm (although Anselm is not named), once the term 'God' is understood, it is seen that the proposition, 'God exists' is self-evident, he distinguishes between things that are self-evident in themselves and also to us, and things that are self-evident in themselves but not to us. In a self-evident proposition, the predicate is included in the essence of the subject, as in 'Man is an animal', so if we know the essence of both predicate and subject, the proposition will be self-evident. If not, the proposition will be self-evident in itself, but not to us. As God is his own existence, subject and predicate are the same, and as we do not know God's essence, the proposition 'God exists,' is not self-evident to us.

For Aquinas, then, if we knew God's essence, we would know that God is a being that must exist. However, we do not know his essence, so, if we wish to prove his existence, we need to use *a posteriori* arguments. Instead of starting with

God, we should start with the things we know, the world God has made and the things it contains, and argue from them to God.

Despite its rejection by Aquinas, the ontological argument continued to interest philosophers and theologians, and in 1641 René Descartes (*Meditations on First Philosophy*, Meditation V), put forward a version of it, arguing that, although it is generally the case that existence must be distinguished from essence, which would suggest that God can be thought of as not existing, in the case of God, his existence can no more be separated from his essence than its having three angles can from the essence of a triangle. And 'from the fact that I cannot think of God except as existing, it follows that existence is inseparable from God'.

The fundamental criticism of the ontological argument was made by Immanuel Kant in his *Critique of Pure Reason* (Book II, Chapter III, Section IV), published in 1781. Kant argues that it confuses logical necessity and necessary existence. If we suppose that a triangle exists, three angles must necessarily exist in it, because having three angles is part of the definition of a triangle. So it is self-contradictory to suppose the existence of the triangle, but not of its three angles. However, it is not self-contradictory to suppose the non-existence of the triangle together with its three angles. Similarly, if we form an *a priori* concept of God that includes existence, it will be self-contradictory to deny that God exists. But no contradiction arises if both God and existence (subject and predicate) are suppressed, for then: 'there is *nothing* at all . . . Annihilate its existence in thought, and you annihilate the thing itself with all its predicates; how then can there be any room for contradiction?' If we build existence into our concept of God, it will be self-contradictory to deny his existence; and, in this sense, he cannot be thought not to exist. But this does not prove that God actually exists.

However, Kant's criticism of the ontological argument goes further: that it wrongly treats existence as an attribute or perfection. Existence is not a concept of something that can be added to the concept of a thing. To say, 'God is', adds no new predicate to the concept of God, but just affirms the existence of the subject, God, with all its predicates. A hundred real pounds contains no more money than a hundred possible pounds. If they did, the concept would not correspond exactly to its object. Therefore, 'In whatever number of predicates . . . I may think a thing, I do not in the least augment the object of my concept by the addition of the statement, this thing exists. Otherwise, not exactly the same, but something more than what was thought in my concept, would exist.'

Thus, existence is not another (and greater) attribute that something has. To say that something exists is to say that there exists in reality an object that corresponds to our concept. The Christian concept of God is of an infinite being and, if he exists, he exists in a completely different way from everything else, because, unlike everything else, which he has created from nothing, he (as Anselm puts it) 'exists through himself', and is the 'one supreme good, utterly self-sufficient, needing nothing, whom all things need for their being and well-being'. But such a being may not exist, and can be thought not to exist; and there is no contradiction involved in doing so.

Anselm now goes on to discuss the attributes that the 'greatest of all beings', who is everything 'it is better to be than not to be', must possess. As nothing good can be missing from 'the highest good, through which every good thing exists', they include omnipotence, mercy, impassibility, justice: in fact, all the attributes of the Christian God. However, even if

Anselm's argument worked, it would only prove the existence of a being than which nothing greater can be thought, not the specifically Christian God. However, for Anselm, who already believes in him, it is the Christian God whose existence he has now proved by the single argument he was seeking.

But there are difficulties with some of God's attributes, while others seem to conflict with each other. For example, how can God be omnipotent, when there are things he cannot do? And how can God be both merciful and impassible? Anselm sets out to resolve these conflicts.

God is believed to be omnipotent, but there are some things, such as lying and causing what is true to be false, that he cannot do. However, these are things that produce no good, and involve weakness not power. They are the work of those whose weakness gives wickedness power over them. But God does nothing through weakness, so nothing has power over him. But how can God be merciful, when he is impassible and does not feel compassion? It is because God is merciful in relation to us, not himself. When he saves and spares sinners, they feel the effects of his mercy, but he feels no compassion.

But how can God's mercy and justice co-exist? A just God should give wicked people their due and punish, not spare, them. It must be accepted that God's mercy flows from his goodness, which is incomprehensible, and that it is better to be good to both the good and the wicked, rather than only to the former. There is no goodness apart from justice, so God acts justly in showing mercy to the wicked. Sinners, therefore, have every reason to love God, because the just are saved through their merits, while they are saved in spite of the fact that they lack them. However, it still puzzles Anselm that God saves some wicked people, but condemns others.

Unlike the things that he has created, God does not cease, or begin, to exist, and he is not limited to place or time; only God can be wholly everywhere at once. What does it mean to say that God is eternal? It means that, in past, present and future, God just is. Past, present and future are in time, but God is outside time altogether. Nothing exists without God, and nothing contains God, who contains all things. He surpasses all eternal things, because their eternity is wholly present to him, but they possess neither the part of their eternity that is still to come, nor the part that is past. God is beyond all these things, because he is present where they have not yet arrived.

All this is very hard to grasp, and Anselm admits that he is at the limits of what human beings are capable of understanding. God is not just that than which nothing greater can be thought, but 'something greater than can be thought'. Like other created beings, Anselm cannot penetrate the 'inaccessible light' in which God dwells, although it is only because of the illumination God gives that he understands anything at all of God. He compares God to the sun. Human beings cannot look directly at the sun, although it is only because of the sun's light that they see anything at all. And how can human beings come close to understanding God when, unlike God, they are composite, changeable things, who are one thing as a whole, but another in their parts. And, of course, because of Adam's sin, human beings are shut out from God's light and covered in darkness.

However, Anselm looks forward to what God, through Jesus, has promised to those who love him. They will be sons of God and joint-heirs with Christ. They can have no idea, in this life, how much they will know and love God in their future life, when, in perfect charity, they will rejoice as much for others as for themselves, and love God more than themselves.

Anselm believed that belief not only precedes understanding, but is essential to it, so although he puts forward a proof of God's existence, he does not seem to have thought that it would convince those who did not already believe in God. Rather, it would help those with pre-existing belief in God to understand the God in whom they believed on the basis of faith. While the ontological argument continues to interest philosophers and theologians, it is difficult not to be persuaded by the criticisms put forward by Aquinas, Hume and Kant. So, the role of Anselm's proof, as of the *Proslogion* as a whole, is as he intended: to help its readers to understand what they believe through faith, by exploring the nature of the Christian God. And even if we find some of Anselm's attempts to reconcile apparent conflicts between God's attributes rather forced, the *Proslogion* is, as Gaunilo acknowledges, 'lucidly and magnificently' argued and 'fragrant with the aroma of devout and holy feeling'.

Some Issues to Consider

- Anselm wanted to find a single argument that would stand by itself as a proof of God's existence. He was not satisfied with the arguments in his *Monologion*, because they were a series of arguments 'chained together'.
- Anselm did not see reason and revelation as mutually exclusive sources of knowledge about God. Human beings had a God-given intellect, which should be used in God's service.
- The *Proslogion* is written in the form of a prayer.
- Anselm thought that people needed to believe in God before they could begin to understand him.
- Anselm defines God as that than which nothing greater can be thought, who must exist in reality, as well as the

understanding, otherwise he would not be that than which nothing greater can be thought.

- He also thought that that than which nothing greater can be thought exists so truly he cannot be thought not to exist.
- Anselm regards existence as an attribute or perfection, which it is greater to possess than not.
- How convincing is Anselm's proof to those who do not already believe in God?
- Do the criticisms of the ontological argument, put forward by Gaunilo, Aquinas, Hume and Kant show that it does not work as a proof of God's existence?
- Was Kant right to say that existence is not an attribute or perfection?
- If Anselm's proof worked, he would only have established the existence of a being than which nothing greater can be thought, not the Christian God.
- How convincing is Anselm's defence of God's omnipotence?
- Can God's mercy and justice co-exist?
- Anselm explains what it means to say that God is eternal: in past, present and future, God just is; they are in time, but he is outside time altogether.
- If God exists, is it possible for human beings to achieve any real understanding of him?
- Gaunilo said that the *Proslogion*, as a whole, was lucidly and magnificently argued and fragrant with the aroma of devout and holy feeling.

Suggestions for Further Reading

Anselm, Proslogion with the Replies of Gaunilo and Anselm, trans. T. Williams, 2001, Indianapolis/Cambridge: Hackett Publishing Company.

Anselm, Monologion and Proslogion with the Replies of Gaunilo and Anselm, trans. T. Williams, 1996, Indianapolis: Hackett Publishing Company.

Basic Writings of Saint Thomas Aquinas, vol. I, ed. A. C. Pegis, 1997, Indianapolis/Cambridge: Hackett Publishing Company (contains the *Summa Theologica*, Part I).

R. Descartes, *Discourse on Method and Meditations on First Philosophy*, ed. D. A Cress, fourth edition, 1998, Indianapolis/Cambridge: Hackett Publishing Company.

B. Davies and B. Leftow (eds), 2004, *The Cambridge Companion to Anselm*, Cambridge: Cambridge University Press.

J. Hick, 1990, *Philosophy of Religion*, fourth edition, Englewood Cliffs, New Jersey: Prentice Hall.

I. Kant, *Critique of Pure Reason*, ed. V. Politis, 1993, London: Everyman.

R. W. Southern, *St Anselm: A Portrait in a Landscape*, 1990, Cambridge: Cambridge University Press.

P. Vardy, 1999, *The Puzzle of God*, revised edition, London: Fount Paperbacks.

Detailed Summary of Anselm's
Proslogion (pp. 2–25)

Prologue (pp. 2–3)

After publishing 'a short work as a pattern of **meditation** on the **rational basis of faith**', which chained together 'many arguments', I began to wonder whether there might be a 'single argument', which would **prove God's existence** (p. 2). At times, I thought I had grasped what I was looking for, but eventually it seemed 'impossible' (p. 2). However, my desire to find such an argument persisted, and then one day it presented itself to me.

I thought that readers might be pleased to read what had delighted me, so I wrote it down as one raising his mind to '**contemplation** of God' and seeking to understand what he believes (p. 2). I called the first of my two works (they did not deserve to be called books, or to have an author's name), '"A pattern for meditation on the rational basis of faith"', and the second, '"Faith seeking **understanding**"' (p. 2). But I was then encouraged by several people, including '**Hugo, the Most Reverend Archbishop of Lyons**', to put my name on them (p. 3). And to 'do so more suitably', I entitled them the *Monologion* and the *Proslogion* (p. 3).

Contents

Chapter I (pp. 4–6)

'Insignificant **mortal**', set aside your 'restless thoughts' to 'make room for God' (p. 4). 'Lord', show me 'where and how to find you' (p. 4). If you are 'everywhere', why do I not see you (p. 4)? I 'long to see you', but you are too 'far away', and I do not know 'where you are' (p. 4). You are my **creator**, who has given me 'every good thing' I have, but I do not know you (pp. 4–5).

Human beings are 'wretched' (p. 5). Once they 'ate the bread of angels (Psalm 78.25)', but now they 'eat the bread of sorrows (Psalm 127.2)' (p. 5). Why did **Adam** 'shut us out from the **light** and cover us with **darkness**', taking away our life and inflicting 'death upon us' (p. 5)? We have gone from 'the **vision of God**' and the 'joy of **immortality**' to the 'terror of death' (p. 5).

When, Lord, 'will you look favourably upon us and hear us', because, without you, 'it goes so badly for us' (pp. 5–6)? And 'without you we can do nothing' (p. 6). Teach me, 'how to seek you, and show yourself to me when I seek' (p. 6). I am grateful, Lord, that you have 'created in me this **image** of you so that I may remember you, think of you, and **love** you' (p. 6). But **sin** has so 'eroded' the image that it needs renewal (p. 6). But, I 'long to understand your truth in some way', because my heart 'believes and loves' your truth (p. 6). I do not 'seek to understand in order to believe'; I believe 'in order to understand'. For I believe that '"Unless I believe, I shall not understand"' (p. 6).

Chapter II (p. 7)

Lord, you give my faith understanding, so enable me to 'understand that you exist as we believe you exist, and that you are what we believe you to be' (p. 7). We believe you are, 'something than which nothing **greater** can be thought' (p. 7). But the **fool** has said, '"There is no God" (Psalm 14.1; 53.1)', so does such a being not exist (p. 7)? But even the fool understands what is meant by 'something than which nothing greater can be thought', even if he does not understand that it exists '[in reality]' (p. 7). It is one thing for an object to exist in the understanding, another to understand that 'it exists in [reality]' (p. 7). When a painter decides what he is going to paint, it is 'in his understanding' (p. 7). But, once the picture has been painted, it is still in his understanding, but he also understands that it exists, 'because he has now painted it' (p. 7). And even the fool must admit that 'something than which nothing greater can be thought' exists in the understanding, because he understands the concept (p. 7). But this concept cannot exist only in the understanding, because, if that is the case, it can also be thought to exist 'in reality', and this 'is greater' (p. 7). If 'that than which a greater cannot be thought exists only in the understanding', then something greater than it '*can* be thought', which is 'clearly impossible' (p. 7). So, there is no doubt that 'something than which a greater cannot be thought exists both in the understanding and in reality' (p. 7).

Chapter III (p. 8)

But this being exists 'so truly', it cannot be 'thought not to exist' (p. 8). Something that 'cannot be thought not to exist' is greater than one that can 'be thought not to exist' (p. 8). If that 'than which a greater cannot be thought' can be thought not to exist, it is 'not that than which a greater cannot be thought': which is a **'contradiction'** (p. 8). Therefore, that than which a greater cannot be thought 'exists so truly that it cannot be thought not to exist' (p. 8).

And this, Lord, 'is you': 'you cannot be thought not to exist' (p. 8). For, if a human mind could think of 'something better', a creature would 'rise above the Creator' (p. 8). Everything that exists, apart from you, 'can be thought not to exist', and exists 'less truly' and 'less greatly' than you (p. 8). So, when the fool denied that you exist, although it is so clear 'to the **rational mind**' that you do, this is because he is 'stupid and a fool' (p. 8).

Chapter IV (pp. 8–9)

But how has the fool said in his heart 'what he could not think' (p. 8)? There are two senses of the word 'think' (p. 8). In one sense, when we think a thing, we think of 'the word that signifies that thing' (p. 8). In another, we 'understand what exactly the thing is' (p. 8). In the first sense, God can be thought not to exist, but 'not at all in the second' (p. 8). No one can understand 'what God is', and think he does not exist (p. 8). To understand that God is 'that than which a greater cannot be thought', is to understand that he exists in such a way that he cannot 'even in thought, fail to exist' (p. 9).

Thank you, Lord, for I 'now understand' what I previously believed 'through your **grace**' (p. 9). Even if I did not want to believe in your existence, 'I could not fail to *understand* that you exist' (p. 9).

Chapter V (p. 9)

Lord, what are you, if not 'the greatest of all beings', **who alone exists through himself**, and '**made all other things from nothing**' (p. 9). Whatever is not this 'is less than the greatest that can be thought': which cannot be thought of you (p. 9). Nothing that is good is missing from 'the **highest good**', through which everything good exists (p. 9). You are '**just**, truthful, happy', and 'whatever it is better to be than not to be' (p. 9).

Chapter VI (pp. 9–10)

It is better to be '**percipient**, **omnipotent**, **merciful**, and **impassible**' than not (p. 9). But how can you see without a **body**, be omnipotent 'if you cannot do everything', or 'be both merciful and impassible' (p. 9)? Things with bodies see, because they have **senses**, but how can you, 'the **highest spirit**', see (p. 9)?

But to see is 'just to know' (p. 9). Whoever sees, knows through 'the appropriate sense'; so, whoever knows 'also in some way perceives' (pp. 9–10). Lord, you do not have a body, but you are 'supremely percipient' as you 'supremely know all things' (p. 10).

Chapter VII (p. 10)

How are you omnipotent, 'if you cannot do everything' (p. 10)? For example, you cannot **lie**, or 'cause what is true to be false' (p. 10).

But is not the ability to do such things 'weakness', rather than power, because they are not '**beneficial**' (p. 10)? So, when we say that someone '"can" do these things', it is not because of his power, but because 'his weakness gives something else power over him' (p. 10). Indeed, we often express ourselves 'loosely', as when we say '"This man is sitting just as that man is doing"', although sitting is not doing anything (p. 10). Similarly, when we say someone has the '"power" to do . . . something that is not beneficial', we mean weakness (p. 10). The more power of this kind someone has, the more power '**wickedness**' has over him (pp. 10–11). But you, Lord, do nothing through weakness, and 'nothing has power over you' (p. 11).

Chapter VIII (p. 11)

How are you 'both merciful and impassible' (p. 11)? To be impassible is not to 'feel **compassion**', so how can you be 'merciful' (p. 11)? And if you are not merciful, how are you able to be 'such a **comfort** to the **sorrowful**' (p. 11)?

Is it because you are 'merciful in relation to us', but not to yourself (p. 11)? When you look favourably 'upon us in our sorrow', we feel the **effect** of your mercy, but 'you do not feel the **emotion**' of it (p. 11). You are merciful, as you 'save the sorrowful' and spare sinners, but you do not experience any 'feeling of compassion' (p. 11).

Chapter IX (pp. 11–13)

How do you 'spare the wicked', if you are 'completely and supremely just', because to do so 'is not just' (p. 11)? What sort of justice is it that gives '**everlasting life** to someone who deserves **eternal death**' (p. 11)?

But your goodness is '**incomprehensible**' (p. 11). Although you are '**supremely just**', you are kind to the wicked, because you are also '**supremely good**' (p. 12). It is better to be good to both the good and the wicked than only to the former. It is easy for us to see why you 'repay the good with good and the evil with evil', but harder for us to understand why you 'give good things to your **evil and guilty creatures**' (p. 12). We can see 'the source of your mercy', but we cannot 'discern it clearly' (p. 12). You are kind to sinners 'out of the fullness of your goodness', but the reason 'lies hidden in the heights of goodness' (p. 12).

How intensely sinners ought 'to love you' (p. 12). The just are '**saved** with the help of their **merits**, sinners despite their merits' (p. 12). So, Lord, spare me 'through your mercy, lest you exact **retribution** through your justice' (p. 12). Although it is hard to understand how your mercy and justice can **co-exist**, we must still believe that they are not opposed to each other, because your mercy flows from your goodness, and 'there is no goodness apart from justice' (p. 12). Indeed, if you are merciful because you are 'supremely good', and supremely good because you are 'supremely just', then you are merciful because you are just (pp. 12-13).

And Lord, if you 'spare the wicked because of your justice', help me to understand 'how it is so' (p. 13). Perhaps, it is because 'it is just for you to be so good that you cannot be understood to be better' (p. 13). What could be more just than this? It would not be so if you were 'good only in punishing and not in sparing' (p. 13). For 'what is not done justly should not be done', so it is 'right to believe that you act justly in being merciful to the wicked' (p. 13).

Chapter X (pp. 13–14)

But it is just for you to punish the wicked, so how is it just that you both punish and spare the wicked? Or do you punish and spare them in different ways? For, when you punish the wicked, that is just, because 'it is in keeping with their merits', but when you spare them, 'it is in keeping with your goodness' (p. 13). In sparing the wicked, you are just, not in relation to them, but 'to yourself' (p. 13). In saving us, 'whom you might justly destroy', you are merciful, not because you feel emotion, but because 'we experience the effect of your mercy' (p. 13). Similarly, you are just, not because you 'give us our due', but because you do what is in keeping with your own supreme goodness (pp. 13–14). So, there is no **'inconsistency'** in your justly punishing and pardoning us (p. 14).

Chapter XI (p. 14)

But, Lord, would it not be just 'in relation to yourself' to pun-ish the wicked (p. 14)? However, it is just for you to be 'so just that you cannot be thought to be more just' (p. 14). And you would not be so just if you only gave good to the good, and 'did not repay the wicked with evil', because to give both the good and the wicked their deserts is 'more just' than doing so 'only for the good' (p. 14). So, Lord, you are just both 'when you punish and when you pardon', because 'only what you will is just' (p. 14). Your mercy comes from your justice, and it is just for you to be so good that you are 'good even in sparing the wicked' (p. 14). But even though we may understand why you save the wicked, it is impossible to understand why, from among the wicked, you save some 'through your supreme goodness', and condemn others 'through your supreme justice' (p. 14).

You are 'percipient, omnipotent, merciful, and impassible . . . living, wise, good, happy, **eternal**': everything that 'it is better to be than not to be' (p. 14).

Chapter XII (pp. 14–15)

You are 'whatever you are', through yourself and not through 'anything else' (p. 14). You are the 'life by which you live, the wisdom by which you are wise, and the very goodness by which you are good' to both the good and the wicked (pp. 14–15).

Chapter XIII (p. 15)

Things subject to the **'law of place or time'** are less than those that are not (p. 15). As 'nothing is greater than you', you are not limited to place or time (p. 15). You 'exist everywhere and always', and you alone are '**unbounded** and eternal' (p. 15)? So, how can this be said of 'other **spirits**' (p. 15)?

You alone are eternal, because you alone do not **cease, or begin, to exist**. But how are you alone unbounded? Is a '**created spirit**' **bounded** when compared to you, but 'unbounded compared to a **material object**' (p. 15)? Only material objects are 'completely bounded': they cannot be 'wholly in one place', and 'somewhere else', at the same time (p. 15). But only you are 'unbounded': 'wholly **everywhere at once**' (p. 15). But 'created spirits' are both 'bounded and unbounded': they can be 'wholly in another place, but not everywhere' (p. 15). So you, Lord, are 'uniquely unbounded and eternal', while other spirits are also 'unbounded and eternal' (p. 15).

Chapter XIV (pp. 15–16)

My soul, have you found what you were seeking? Have you found that God is that 'than which nothing better can be thought', that he is 'life itself', and 'exists always and everywhere' (p. 15)? If not, how is God the one that you have found and 'understood with such certain truth' (pp. 15–16)? If it has found you, Lord, why does my soul not 'perceive you' (p. 16)?

If it has seen light and truth, it has seen you, but, if it has not seen you, it has not seen either. But, perhaps it saw light and truth, but saw you 'only in part', not as you '"really are" (1 John 3.2)' (p. 16).

Lord, tell my soul what you are 'besides what it has seen', for it sees only 'darkness' beyond what it has already seen; or rather, as there is '"no darkness" (1 John 1.5)' in you, it cannot see more, because of its own darkness (p. 16). But why is this? Is it because it is 'overwhelmed by your **vastness**' (p. 16)? From your light, 'flashes every truth that enlightens the rational mind'; and in your truth is 'everything that is true' (p. 16). It sees everything that has been created, and 'how it was all created from nothing' (p. 16). It is 'more than any creature can understand' (p. 16).

Chapter XV (pp. 16–17)

Lord, you are not only that than which 'a greater cannot be thought'; you are 'something greater than can be thought' (p. 16). For, as it is possible to think that such a being exists, if that being is not you, 'it is possible to think something greater than you': but that 'is impossible' (pp. 16–17).

Chapter XVI (p. 17)

No other being can penetrate 'the "**inaccessible** light in which you dwell" (1 Timothy 6.16)' (p. 17). It is 'too much for me' (p. 17). But what I see, I see because of it, just as a 'weak eye' sees by the sun's light, even though it cannot look directly at the sun (p. 17). So, 'the **eye of my soul**' is dazzled by that 'supreme and inaccessible light', which is so far from me, while I am 'so close' to it (p. 17). Lord, you are 'far from my sight', while I am 'present to yours' (p. 17). You are **wholly present** everywhere, but I do not see you (p. 17). In you, '"I have my being" (Acts 17.28)', but I cannot enter your presence (p. 17). I do not see you, even though you are 'within me and all around me' (p. 17).

Chapter XVII (p. 17)

Lord, as you are 'hidden from my **soul** in your light', it lives in 'darkness and misery' (p. 17). It is unable to see your '**beauty**', hear your '**harmony**', perceive your '**fragrance**', know your '**savour**', or sense your '**softness**' (p. 17). You possess these qualities in your own '**ineffable** way', and have imparted them to 'the things you created' (p. 17). But my soul's senses have been 'dulled' by the 'weakness of sin' (p. 17).

Chapter XVIII (pp. 18–19)

My soul sought 'satisfaction', but it is 'overwhelmed by need' (p. 18). I tried to 'rise to the light of God', but fell back 'into my own darkness' (p. 18). Indeed, we fell long ago 'in him "in whom we all sinned" (Romans 5.12)' (p. 18). Help me, Lord, '"because of your goodness" (Psalm 27.8–9)' (p. 18). Let my soul have strength, so that it may 'strive with all its understanding to reach you' (p. 18).

What are you, Lord? You are 'wisdom', 'truth', 'happiness', 'eternity' and 'every true good' (p. 18). But how can you be 'all these things' (p. 18)? Are they **parts** of you (p. 18)? However, that which consists of parts 'is not completely one', and can be 'broken up' in fact or understanding (p. 18). But this is not so with you, 'than whom nothing better can be thought' (p. 18). In fact, you are '**unity itself**', and cannot be 'divided by any understanding' (p. 18). Life, wisdom 'and the rest' are not 'parts of you', but 'all one', and each is 'what the rest are' (p. 18). And as you have no parts, neither does your eternity; so 'no part of you or of your eternity exists at a certain place or time' (pp. 18–19). You exist 'as a whole in every place', and your eternity 'exists as a whole always' (p. 19).

Chapter XIX (p. 19)

Lord, by your eternity, 'you have been, and are, and will be' (p. 19). But how does your eternity 'exist as a whole always' (p. 19)?

Is it the case that 'nothing of your eternity is in the past in such a way that it no longer exists', while none is in the future 'as if it did not exist already' (p. 19)? So, we should understand that 'yesterday, today, and tomorrow you *are*' (p. 19). Indeed, even this way of expressing it misses the point that 'you are simply **outside time altogether**' (p. 19). Yesterday, today and tomorrow are 'merely in time' (p. 19). But you, although 'nothing exists without you, do not exist in a place or a time' (p. 19). Nothing 'contains you, but you contain all things' (p. 19).

Chapter XX (pp. 19–20)

You are 'before and beyond all things' (p. 19). But how are you 'beyond those things that will have no end' (p. 19)?

Is it because they cannot 'exist without you', whereas you would not 'exist any less even if they return to nothingness' (p. 19). Also, they can be 'thought to have an end', but you cannot (p. 19). And what does not, in any sense, have an end is 'beyond what does' (pp. 19–20). Further, you 'surpass' all eternal things, because their eternity is 'wholly present to you', but they do not possess the 'part of their eternity' yet to come, in the same way that they 'no longer possess the part that is past' (p. 20). You are beyond them, because you are always present where 'they have not yet arrived' (p. 20).

Chapter XXI (p. 20)

Your eternity 'contains even the very **ages of time**' (p. 20). You are so great, Lord, because 'all things are full of you and are in you'; yet 'you have no **spatial extension**' (p. 20).

Chapter XXII (pp. 20–1)

You alone, Lord, are what and who you are. For, whatever is one thing as a whole, but another 'in its parts', and contains 'something **changeable**', is not 'entirely what it is' (p. 20). Whatever started to exist 'out of **non-existence**' can be thought 'not to exist' (p. 20). It returns to non-existence, unless it 'subsists through some other being' (p. 20). And something with a past that no longer exists, and a future that does not exist, 'does not exist in a strict and absolute sense' (p. 20).

But you do exist strictly and absolutely, because you have 'only a present', and 'cannot be thought not to exist at any time' (pp. 20–1). You are the 'one supreme good, utterly **self-sufficient**, needing nothing, whom all things need for their being and well-being' (p. 21).

Chapter XXIII (p. 21)

This good is you, Lord, and 'your **Son**' (p. 21). For there cannot be anything 'greater or less than you, in the **Word** by which you utter yourself' (p. 21). He is the 'same truth' that you are (p. 21). And this good is the 'one love' that you and your Son share, and 'who **proceeds** from you both', 'the **Holy Spirit**' (p. 21). This love is not unequal to you or your Son, and 'is not other than you', because he proceeds from you (p. 21). Thus, whatever each of you is 'individually', that is what the 'whole

Trinity' of **Father**, Son, and Holy Spirit is (p. 21). Each of you individually is nothing other than 'the supremely simple unity and the supremely united simplicity', which cannot be 'different from itself': the 'complete, one, total, and unique good' (p. 21).

Chapter XXIV (pp. 21–2)

O my soul, try to understand 'what sort of good this is', and its greatness (p. 21). Particular goods cause delight, but this good 'contains the joyfulness of all goods'; and it is not just the sort of joy we find in **'created things'** (pp. 21–2). For the creator created life, and brings **salvation**; so, if we delight in 'delightful things', how much more do we delight 'in him who made those delightful things' (p. 22).

Chapter XXV (pp. 22–4)

Those who enjoy this good will have 'everything they want' (p. 22). So, we must love 'the one good, in which are all good things' (p. 22). Whatever you 'long for' or 'love' is there (p. 22).

If it is beauty, '"the righteous will shine like the sun" (Matthew 13.43)' (p. 22). If it is swiftness or strength, '"they will be like the angels of God" (Matthew 22.30)' (p. 22). If it is 'a long and healthy life', '"the **righteous** will live for ever" (Wisdom 5.15)' (p. 22). If satisfaction, they will be satisfied when '"the glory of God has appeared" (Psalm 17.13)' (p. 22). If wisdom, God's wisdom will 'show itself to them' (p. 23). If friendship, they will love God 'more than themselves and one another through God' (p. 23). If **concord**, they will have no will 'but the will of God' (p. 23). If power, they will be 'omnipotent' through their wills, as God is (p. 23). If wealth and honour, God will '"set his good and faithful servants over many things" (Matthew 25.21, 23)', and they will be '"**sons of God**" (Matthew 5.9)' (p. 23). And they will be '"**joint-heirs with Christ**" (Romans 8.17)' (p. 23). They will have '**true security**', which 'the loving God' will never remove, against their will, from 'those who love him' (p. 23).

O 'human heart', how you would rejoice to have 'all these things' (p. 23). And you would rejoice if 'someone else whom you loved' had them (p. 23). Indeed, in that '**perfect charity**' of **angels** and human beings, 'each one will rejoice for each of the others' as for himself (p. 23). And, as everyone in that 'perfect happiness' will love God 'incomparably more' than himself, so everyone will rejoice 'inconceivably more' in God's happiness than his own (pp. 23–4). They will love God so much that their 'whole heart, mind, and soul' will be too small for 'the greatness of their love' and 'the fullness of their joy' (p. 24).

Chapter XXVI (pp. 24–5)

Lord, is this the joy 'of which you tell us through your Son' (p. 24)? Even when our whole beings are full of joy, there will still remain 'joy beyond measure' (p. 24). Is this the joy 'your servants' will have when they '"enter into the joy of the Lord" (Matthew 25.21)' (p. 24)? Lord, in this life, we have not seen or heard 'how much they will love and know you in that life' (p. 24).

O God, 'I pray that I will know and love you that I might rejoice in you' (p. 24). Let knowledge and love of you 'grow in me here' (p. 24). Through your Son, you 'counsel us' to ask, and promise that we will receive (pp. 24–5). O God, I ask to receive, '"that my joy may be full"' (p. 25). In the meantime, let me think, speak of, and love it; and let my 'my whole being long for it', until I '"enter into the joy of my Lord", who is God, **Three in One** (Romans 1.25)' (p. 25).

Detailed Summary of Gaunilo's *Reply on Behalf of the Fool* (pp. 28–33)

One who doubts that there is a being 'than which nothing greater can be thought' is told his existence is proved thus (p. 28). To be able to doubt this being's existence is to have it in the understanding, since 'he understands what is said' (p. 28). And what he understands must also 'exist in reality', because that is greater than existing only in the understanding (p. 28). If it exists only in the understanding, that which is 'greater than everything else' would not be, which would be a 'contradiction' (p. 28). So that which is 'greater than everything else' must exist 'in reality', as well as in the understanding (p. 28).

But one response to the point that it exists in my understanding, because I understand it, is that my understanding contains 'any number of false things', which I understand, but which have 'no real existence' (p. 28). So, it needs to be established that 'this being' cannot be thought of in the same way as 'false or doubtful things', and that I cannot have it in my understanding without 'comprehending in genuine knowledge the fact that it actually exists' (p. 28).

But this would mean that there would be 'no distinction' between having a thing in the understanding, and then later understanding that it exists, as is the case with, for example, a painting, which 'exists first in the mind of the painter and then in the finished work' (pp. 28–9). It also seems impossible to accept that this being 'cannot be thought not to exist'

(p. 29). Even God can be thought not to exist. I need proof that this being only needs to be thought of for 'the understanding to perceive with certainty that it undoubtedly exists' (p. 29). It is not enough to say that it exists in my understanding, because I understand many things that are 'doubtful or even false' (p. 29).

The **analogy** of the painter does not support the argument (p. 29). Before it is painted, the picture is contained 'in the craft of the painter', which is 'part of his intelligence' (p. 29). So, some things belong to the mind itself, and, when the **intellect**, on hearing about something, sees that it is true, it can distinguish that truth 'from the intellect that grasps it' (p. 29).

When I hear the expression, 'that which is greater than everything else that can be thought' (which, it is claimed, can only be God), I can no more think of it in terms of anything I know than 'I can think of God himself'; and, for this 'very reason': I 'can also think of him as not existing' (pp. 29–30). I do not know the thing itself, nor can I 'form an idea of it on the basis of something like it' (p. 30). Indeed, it is said that there is nothing like it (p. 30). If I hear about a man I do not know, I can think of him in terms of men in general. Now, I might have been given false information, and this particular man might not exist. However, I would have been thinking of him on the basis of 'a real thing': what men are in general (p. 30).

But when I am told about 'God', or 'something greater than everything else', I cannot have it in my understanding in the same way (p. 30). There is no 'real thing', such as men in general, on which to base my thinking about him; I can think about him only 'on the basis of the word' itself (p. 30). However, this involves the word's meaning; and we do not know what this word 'customarily' means (p. 30). Instead, we have to think of its 'impression' on the mind, and try to 'imagine' what it means (p. 30). And it would be surprising if we reached the truth about anything in that way. So much, then, for the claim that 'that **supreme nature** already exists in my understanding' (p. 30).

There is a further argument: that this thing, which has already been proved to exist in the understanding, 'necessarily exists in reality, since if it did not, everything that exists in reality would be greater than it' (pp. 30–1). I do not deny that 'this thing exists in my understanding', even though it cannot be thought of, 'on the basis of the true nature of anything whatever' (p. 31). However, there is no way to derive the conclusion that it exists 'in reality' from its existence in the understanding (p. 31).

As for the argument that this thing must exist, because otherwise that which is greater than everything else would not be, I deny that it is 'greater than any real thing' (p. 31). I also deny that 'it exists at all', except in so far as existence can be ascribed to something 'completely unknown', which the mind tries to imagine 'on the basis of a word' (p. 31). The so-called proof that this thing is greater than everything else does not show that it exists 'in actual fact' (p. 31). Indeed, I do not accept that it exists in my understanding, even as 'doubtful and uncertain things' do (p. 31). I need to be certain that it really exists somewhere before the fact of its being greater than everything else convinces me that 'it also subsists in itself' (p. 31).

There are those who maintain that, somewhere in the ocean, there is a '**Lost Island**', 'superior' to any other human habitation (p. 31). I can understand this story. But somebody might then argue that this island's real existence cannot be doubted. It exists in the understanding, and, since it is 'more excellent' to exist in reality than only in the understanding, it must exist in reality (pp. 31–2). And if it does not, any land that does exist is greater. But to accept this argument, I would need to be convinced that 'its excellence exists in my understanding as a thing that truly and undoubtedly exists and not in any way like something false or uncertain' (p. 32).

The next assertion is that this 'greater being' cannot fail to exist, 'even in thought'; otherwise, it would 'not be greater than everything else' (p. 32). To this, my response is that first I require proof that 'some superior being' exists, which is greater and better than all others, and from which, 'all of the qualities that that which is greater and better than all other things must necessarily possess' can be proved (p. 32). Instead of saying that the '**highest thing**' 'cannot be *thought* not to exist', it would be better to say that 'it cannot be *understood* not to exist', or be capable of not existing (p. 32). Strictly, false things cannot be understood, although they can be thought.

I certainly know that I exist, but I also know I can fail to exist. I know that God exists and 'cannot fail to exist' (p. 32). I do not know whether I can think I do not exist, while knowing certainly that I do. But if it is possible, I can do the same for anything else I certainly know to exist. And, if not, it is not only God 'who cannot be thought not to exist' (p. 32).

The rest of the book (the *Proslogion*) is 'lucidly and magnificently' argued, and 'full of so much that is useful, and fragrant with the aroma of devout and holy feeling' (p. 32). It should not be 'belittled' because of the contents of the opening chapters, which are understood, but not 'compellingly argued' (p. 33). The arguments need to be 'demonstrated more solidly' (p. 33).

Detailed Summary of Anselm's *Reply to Gaunilo* (pp. 36–46)

The one who 'takes me to task' is not a fool, but a **Christian**; so I shall reply to the Christian (p. 36).

You say that 'something than which a greater cannot be thought' is not in the understanding any differently from something which cannot be 'thought according to the true nature of anything at all' (p. 36). You say, too, that it does not follow that that than which a greater cannot be thought exists 'in reality', just because it exists in the understanding (p. 36). But if it cannot be understood or thought, and does not exist in either thought or understanding, God is 'not that than which a greater cannot be thought'; or, if he is neither understood nor thought, he 'exists neither in the understanding nor in thought' (p. 36). Your faith should tell you that this is not so. That than which a greater cannot be thought is understood and thought, and exists 'in the understanding and in thought' (p. 36).

You maintain that it does not follow from the fact that this **concept** is understood that it exists in the understanding, and that its existence in reality does not follow from its existence in the understanding. But if it can be thought to exist, 'it must necessarily exist' (p. 36). It cannot be thought of 'as beginning to exist', whereas things which can be thought to exist, but in fact do not, can be thought of in this way (p. 36). So, it is not the case that it can be thought to exist, but does not actually do so: if 'it can be thought to exist', it **exists 'necessarily'** (p. 36).

Indeed, if it can be thought at all, it 'necessarily exists' (p. 37). Nobody who doubts the existence of such a being doubts that, if it did exist, it would be 'unable to fail to exist either in reality or in the understanding' (p. 37). If it could, it would not be that than which a greater cannot be thought. But something that can be thought, but which does not actually exist, could, if it existed, 'fail to exist either in reality or in the understanding' (p. 37).

Something that can be thought, but does not exist, would not, if it did exist, 'be that than which a greater cannot be thought' (p. 37). So, if it can be 'thought at all', it exists (p. 37). Further, if something does not 'exist everywhere and always', it can be thought 'not to exist anywhere or at any time' (p. 37). Even with **time and the universe**, the 'whole of time does not always exist', and the whole universe 'is not everywhere' (p. 37). Even if they actually exist, things that do not exist 'as a whole in all places and at all times' can be thought 'not to exist' (p. 37). But, if it exists, that than which a greater cannot be thought, 'cannot be thought not to exist' (p. 37). If it could, it is not that than which a greater cannot be thought.

Can such a being be 'thought and understood', and can it 'exist in thought or in the understanding' (p. 38)? You might say that it is not *fully* understood', but this would be like saying that someone, who cannot look 'directly' at the sun, does not 'see the light of day', which is the sun (p. 38). If someone hears 'the words "that than which a greater cannot be thought"', he understands them (p. 38). You might argue that it does not follow from its existing in the understanding that 'it is understood' (p. 38). But, if it is understood, it must exist 'in the understanding', because this is how we understand things (p. 38).

And if such a being 'exists only in the understanding', it both is, and is not, that than which a greater cannot be thought (p. 38). But if it can be thought actually to exist, that is greater than existence in the understanding alone. Therefore, it surely follows that it cannot just exist 'in the understanding', because, if it does, 'it is that than which a greater *can* be thought' (pp. 38–9).

What about your 'Lost Island' argument (p. 39)? Well, if anyone can identify anything to which the 'inference in my argument' can be applied, except 'that than which a greater cannot be thought', I will 'find and give to him that Lost Island' (p. 39). But if someone argues that 'that than which a greater cannot be thought' does not exist, either he is 'not thinking at all', or he will in fact be thinking of 'something that cannot be thought not to exist' (p. 39).

Perhaps, you would say that 'it cannot be *understood* not to exist' (p. 39). But '*thought*' is 'more correct', for otherwise you might argue that 'nothing that exists can be understood not to exist', because it would be 'false' (pp. 39–40). Even if something that actually exists cannot be '*understood* not to exist', everything, apart from that which 'exists in the highest degree', can be '*thought*' not to (p. 40). Everything with a 'beginning or end', which consists of parts, or which 'does not exist always and everywhere as a whole', can be thought of as not existing (p. 40).

You can think you do not exist, even though you know that you do; and we can imagine things that we can think of as existing, which do not, and vice-versa. But we cannot think of something as 'existing and not existing at the same time' (p. 40). Thus, in one sense, we can think of things that we know to exist as not existing. But this is not the case with 'that than which a greater cannot be thought'; so, 'God alone cannot be thought not to exist' (p. 40).

You also say that my argument is that 'that which is greater than everything else' exists in the understanding, and, if it does, exists in reality as well, because otherwise it would not be 'greater than everything else' (p. 41). This is not my argument. 'That which is greater than everything else' is not the same as 'that than which nothing greater can be thought' (p. 41). It is easy to refute one who denies that the latter exists in reality, or who argues that it can be 'thought not to exist' (p. 41). Even if it exists, whatever can be thought not to exist, is 'not that than which a greater cannot be thought'; and if it does not exist, *even if it were to exist*, it would not be that than which a greater cannot be thought (p. 41). So, it is clear that that than which a greater cannot be thought exists, is 'not capable of not existing', and cannot be thought not to exist (p. 41).

But it is not the same with 'what is said to be greater than everything else' (p. 41). It is not obvious that something which can be thought not to exist is not 'greater than everything else that exists'; nor is it obvious that it is the same as that than which a greater cannot be thought; nor is it beyond question that there could not exist more than one thing that was greater than everything else that exists (p. 41). If somebody said that something exists, which is 'greater than everything else that exists', but which can be thought not to exist, and that 'something greater than it can be thought', it would obviously not be 'greater than everything else that exists'. Nor would it be that than which a greater cannot be thought (pp. 41–2). With that which is greater than everything else that exists, 'another **premise**' is needed, but this is not the case with that than which a greater cannot be thought (p. 42). That than which a greater cannot be thought 'proves things about itself', which that which is said to be greater than everything else does not (p. 42). That than which a greater cannot be thought 'cannot be understood as anything other than the one thing that is greater than everything else' (p. 42).

You make the point that 'false or doubtful things' can be

understood and can exist in the understanding (p. 42). All I was doing was attempting to show that that than which a greater cannot be thought 'exists in the understanding, *in some way or other*', before going on to 'determine whether it exists only in the understanding, like a false thing, or also in reality, like a real thing' (p. 42). If false and doubtful things are 'understood, and exist in the understanding', in that they are understood when heard, 'there is no reason that the being I was discussing could not be understood or exist in the understanding' (p. 42). Your arguments are not 'consistent' (p. 42). You say that you would understand what somebody meant if they said false things, but also that, if what you heard is not held in thought, 'in the same way that false things are', you would not say that you 'think it and have it in your thought', but that you 'understand it and have it in your understanding', as 'you cannot think this thing without understanding it, that is, comprehending in genuine knowledge that it exists in reality' (pp. 42–3). How can it be consistent to say that false things are 'understood in some sense', and that to understand is to comprehend in genuine knowledge that something exists (p. 43)? If it is possible to understand 'false things' in some way, and 'your definition of understanding' applies only 'to some cases of understanding', you should not have criticized me 'for saying that that than which a greater cannot be thought is understood and exists in the understanding even before it was certain that it exists in reality' (p. 43).

Your next point is that it is difficult to accept that that than which a greater cannot be thought 'cannot be thought not to exist in the way that even God can be thought not to exist' (p. 43). Does it really make sense to deny the existence of something that is understood, because it is said to be 'the same as something', the existence of which is denied, because it is not understood (p. 43)? It is not possible to accept that anybody would deny the existence of that than which a greater cannot be thought, because he denied the existence of God, about whom he was not thinking anyway. If, because he does not completely understand it, somebody denies the existence of that than which a greater cannot be thought, would it not be more straightforward to prove the existence of something, which is to some extent understood, than of something not understood at all? It made sense to speak of 'that than which a greater cannot be thought', which could be understood to some degree, than of 'God', which might not be (p. 43).

You claim that that than which a greater cannot be thought is not like a picture, which has not yet been painted, and which exists in the painter's understanding. But you miss the point. I did not introduce this example, because I thought it was the same 'sort of thing' as that than which a greater cannot be thought, but to 'show that something exists in the understanding that would not be understood to exist [in reality]' (p. 44).

You state that you cannot think of that than which a greater cannot be thought in relation to 'some thing that you know by **genus** or **species**' (p. 44). But 'lesser goods', by being good, resemble greater ones, so it is possible to make inferences about that than which a greater cannot be thought from things 'than which a greater can be thought' (p. 44). For example, if something with a beginning and an end is good, something that begins, but never ends, is better; and 'something that has neither beginning nor end is better still' (p. 44). And something which does not need 'to change or move' is still better, irrespective of whether or not it actually exists (p. 44). So, we can infer that than which a greater cannot be thought from things than which a greater can be thought. And any '**orthodox**

Christian' who thinks otherwise should recall Romans 1.20, which tells us that God's 'everlasting power and divinity' have been 'clearly seen through the things that have been made' (p. 44).

Even if it were the case that that than which a greater cannot be thought 'cannot be thought or understood', it would not be wrong to say that 'the expression' itself could be (p. 44). A thing can be said to be 'unthinkable', although it 'cannot be thought' (p. 45). In the same way, the expression, 'that than which a greater cannot be thought', can be thought and understood, although 'the thing itself' cannot be (p. 45). And a person, who denies its existence, must be thinking and understanding his 'denial' (p. 45). Further, it is possible to think and understand something which 'cannot fail to exist', and a person, who is thinking of that than which a greater cannot be thought, must be thinking of something that cannot 'fail to exist'; and so 'the thing that he is thinking exists necessarily' (p. 45).

The proof that I have put forward is 'a quite conclusive one' (p. 45). When that than which a greater cannot be thought is 'understood or thought', it is 'necessarily proved both to exist in reality and to be whatever we ought to believe about the divine nature' (p. 45). And our belief about this is that it is everything which it is 'better to be than not': 'eternal' and 'goodness itself' (p. 45).

I thank you for both your praise and your criticism. You praised what you agreed with, and your criticisms were given 'not from ill will but in a friendly spirit' (p. 46).

Overview

The following section is a chapter-by-chapter overview of Anselm's *Proslogion*, Gaunilo's *Reply on Behalf of the Fool* and Anselm's *Reply to Gaunilo*, designed for quick reference to the detailed summary above. Readers may also find this overview section helpful for revision.

The italicised sub-headings in Gaunilo's *Reply on Behalf of the Fool* and Anselm's *Reply to Gaunilo* have been included to make the development of their arguments easier to follow.

Overview of Anselm's Proslogion *(pp. 2–25)*

Prologue *(pp. 2–3)*

Anselm refers to his *Monologion* as a work that brings together a number of arguments for God's existence, but with which he was not satisfied, because he wanted to find one convincing argument. After much thought, he came up with the one in the *Proslogion*. He explains that he is only presenting it to a wider public, because others have persuaded him to do so. He has written the book as one who is seeking to understand what he believes.

Chapter I *(pp. 4–6)*

The *Proslogion* is in the form of a prayer. Anselm begins by asking God to show him where to find him. God is his creator, who has given him everything good, but he does not know him. Human beings had once enjoyed the vision of God and immortality, but, as a result of Adam's sin, are mortal and shut out from the light of God. They can do nothing without

God, and so need God to show them how to seek him. It is as well that they are created in God's image, as this gives them some knowledge of God, but it has been worn down by sin. Anselm longs to understand God's truth, but he is not seeking to understand in order to believe in God. He knows that, in order to understand God, he first needs to believe in him.

Chapter II (p. 7)

To give his faith understanding, he asks God to help him to understand that God is as he is believed to be, which is something than which a greater cannot be thought. This has not stopped the fool saying that there is no God, but even he understands what is meant by something than which a greater cannot be thought, although he does not understand that it actually exists. The existence of an object in the understanding, and understanding that it actually exists, are different things. When a painter decides to paint a picture, it exists first in his understanding, but, once painted, he also understands that it exists in reality. And even the fool must admit that something than which a greater cannot be thought exists in the understanding, because he understands the concept. But this concept cannot exist only in the understanding because, if it did, it could also be thought to exist in reality, which would be greater. And, if that than which a greater cannot be thought existed only in the understanding, something greater than it could be thought. But this would be impossible. So, Anselm concludes that something than which a greater cannot be thought exists both in the understanding and in reality.

Chapter III (p. 8)

Anselm goes on to argue that that than which a greater cannot be thought exists so truly that it cannot be thought not to
exist, because something that cannot be thought not to exist
is greater than something that can be thought not to exist.
Indeed, if that than which a greater cannot be thought can be
thought not to exist, it is not that than which a greater cannot be thought, which would be a contradiction. Therefore,
it exists so truly that it cannot be thought not to exist. He
concludes that that than which a greater cannot be thought,
and which cannot be thought not to exist, is God. Everything
else that exists can be thought not to exist, because it exists
less truly than God. When the fool denies God's existence, it
is because he is a fool.

Chapter IV (pp. 8–9)

Anselm asks God how the fool can believe something that he
cannot think. It is because there are two senses of the word
'think': to think of the word that signifies the thing, and to
think of the thing itself. God can be thought not to exist, in
the first sense, but not the second, because no one can understand what God is, and think he does not exist. To understand
that God is that than which a greater cannot be thought is to
understand that he exists in such a way that he cannot fail to
exist, even in thought. Anselm thanks God for enabling him
to understand what he had previously believed through grace.
Even if he did not want to believe in God's existence, he could
not now fail to understand that he exists.

Chapter V (p. 9)

As the greatest of all beings, God alone is self-existing, and created everything else from nothing. So, everything else is not like God, and is less than the greatest that can be thought. God, the highest good, through whom everything good exists, himself lacks nothing good. He is whatever it is better to be than not to be.

Chapter VI (pp. 9–10)

Anselm considers God's attributes and how it is better to be percipient, omnipotent, merciful and impassible than not. But he wonders how God can see without a body and senses; be omnipotent without being able to do everything; or be both merciful and impassible. He concludes that seeing is just knowing so God, who knows everything, sees by knowing.

Chapter VII (p. 10)

He asks God how he can be omnipotent, when he cannot do everything, such as lying or causing what is true to be false. It is because, as they bring no benefits, doing so involves weakness, not power. People do such things, because their weakness gives something else power over them. The more of this kind of power they have, the more power wickedness has over them. God, however, does nothing through weakness, and nothing has power over him.

Chapter VIII (p. 11)

Anselm asks God how he can be both merciful and impassible, as being impassible means not feeling compassion. He thinks it is because God is merciful in relation to us, but not himself. So, when he is merciful, he looks favourably on sorrowing human beings and saves them, and spares sinners; they feel the effects of his mercy, but he does not experience any feeling of compassion.

Chapter IX (pp. 11–13)

If God is supremely just, it is hard to understand why he spares the wicked. However, God's goodness is incomprehensible. He is supremely good as well as supremely just, and it is better to be good to both the good and the wicked than only to the former. Sinners have every reason to love God, as the just are saved through their merits, while they are saved, despite lacking them. It is not easy to see how mercy and justice can co-exist, but it must be accepted, as God's mercy flows from his goodness, and there can be no goodness apart from justice. He is also so good that he cannot be understood to be better, which would not be the case if he were good only at punishing and not sparing. Therefore, it is right to believe that he acts justly in showing mercy to the wicked.

Chapter X (pp. 13–14)

Although it is just for God to punish the wicked, it does not seem just that he both punishes and spares them. Perhaps, it is just for him to punish the wicked, which is in keeping with their merits, but also to spare them, which is in keeping with his goodness. When God spares the wicked he is being just, not to them, but to himself. In saving such human beings he is merciful, not because he feels emotion, but because human beings experience the effects of his mercy, and doing so is in keeping with his own supreme goodness. Anselm concludes that there is no inconsistency in God both punishing and pardoning human beings.

Chapter XI (p. 14)

Anselm still considers that God would be just to himself if he punished the wicked, but accepts that it is just for God to be so just that he cannot be thought more just. He would not be, if he only gave good to the good, and did not repay the wicked with evil. Giving both the good and the wicked their deserts is more just than doing so only for the good. God is just both when he punishes and pardons, because only what he wills is just. Indeed, his mercy comes from his justice, and it is just for him to be so good that he is good even when he spares the wicked. However, although it is understandable that he saves the wicked, it is hard to understand why he saves some wicked people, but condemns others. However, God is percipient, omnipotent, merciful, impassible, living, wise, good, happy, eternal and everything that it is better to be than not to be.

Chapter XII (pp. 14–15)

God is what he is through himself, not anything else. He is the life by which he lives, the wisdom by which he is wise, and the goodness by which he is good to both the good and the wicked.

Chapter XIII (p. 15)

Things subject to laws of place and time are less than those that are not. Nothing is greater than God, who does not cease, or begin, to exist, and who is not limited to place or time. But Anselm wonders about the situation of created spirits, and whether they are bounded, compared to God, but unbounded, compared to material objects. He concludes that only material objects, which cannot be wholly in one place and somewhere else at the same time, are wholly bounded. Created spirits are both bounded and unbounded: they can be wholly in more than one place, but not everywhere. Only God can be wholly everywhere at once, so, while other spirits are unbounded and eternal, God is uniquely unbounded and eternal.

Chapter XIV (pp. 15–16)

Anselm wonders whether his soul has discovered that God is that than which nothing better can be thought; is life itself; and exists always and everywhere; and, if it has, why it does not see God. Perhaps, his soul has only partly seen God. He wants God to enlighten his soul, which still sees only darkness, not because there is darkness in God, but because of its own darkness. The problem is that, although God's truth contains everything that is true, because God sees everything that has been created, and how it was created from nothing, it is more than mere creatures can understand.

Chapter XV (pp. 16–17)

God is not only that than which a greater cannot be thought, but something greater than can be thought. It is possible to think that such a being exists, but if that being is not God, it is possible to think of something greater than God, which is impossible.

Chapter XVI (p. 17)

While no other being can penetrate the inaccessible light in which God dwells, Anselm acknowledges he sees as much as he does because of it. God is far from his sight, although he is present in God's and God is everywhere. Anselm cannot enter God's presence, even though it is in God that he has his being, and God is within and all around him.

Chapter XVII (p. 17)

As God is hidden from Anselm's soul, which cannot experience his beauty, harmony, fragrance, savour or softness, it lives in darkness and misery. God has these qualities in his own ineffable way, and has imparted them to the things he has created. But the senses of Anselm's soul have been dulled by sin.

Chapter XVIII (pp. 18–19)

Anselm regrets that fact that humanity fell through Adam's sin. He asks God to strengthen his soul, so that it can strive to reach him. He asks how God can be wisdom, truth, happiness, eternity and every true good. They cannot be part of God, because something consisting of parts is not completely one. God, by contrast, is that than whom nothing better can be thought, and is unity itself. God's attributes are not parts of him, but all one, each being what the rest are.

Chapter XIX (p. 19)

By his eternity, God has been, is, and will be. Anselm considers how God's eternity can exist as a whole, always. What human beings need to grasp is that, in past, present and future, God just is. Past, present and future are merely in time, but God is outside it altogether. Nothing exists without God, who does not exist in a place or a time. Nothing contains God, who contains all things.

Chapter XX (pp. 19–20)

God is before and beyond all things, but it is difficult to understand how he is beyond things that will have no end. It could be because such things cannot exist without him, and can be thought to have an end, while he cannot. God surpasses all eternal things, because their eternity is wholly present to him, and they possess neither the part of their eternity that is still to come, nor the part that is past. God is beyond these things, because he is always present where they have not yet arrived.

Chapter XXI (p. 20)

God's eternity contains the ages of time. God is so great, because all things are full of him and are in him, although he has no spatial extension.

Chapter XXII (pp. 20–21)

Only God is what and who he is, unlike changeable things, which are one thing as a whole, but another in their parts.

Things that started to exist out of non-existence can be thought not to exist and, unless they subsist through some other being, return to non-existence. Their past no longer exists, and their future does not exist, so they do not exist strictly and absolutely. However, God does, because he has only a present, and cannot be thought not to exist. He is the one supreme and utterly self-sufficient good, upon whom all things depend for their being and well-being.

Chapter XXIII (p. 21)

God and Jesus are this supreme and utterly self-sufficient good, as there cannot be anything greater or less than God in his Word, by whom he expresses himself. The Holy Spirit, who is not unequal to God or Jesus, proceeds from them both. Whatever each of them is individually, that is what the whole Trinity of Father, Son and Holy Spirit is. Each, individually, is nothing other than the supremely simple unity and the supremely united simplicity, which is one complete, total, and unique good.

Chapter XXIV (pp. 21–2)

Anselm urges his soul to try to understand the sort of good that God is. Particular goods may cause delight, but God contains the joy of all goods. It is not like the joy found in created things. God created life, and brings salvation, so, if people delight in created things, how much more should they delight in the God who made them.

Chapter XXV (pp. 22–4)

Those who enjoy this good will have all that they want, and so must love the one good, in which they will find all good things. They will be sons of God and joint-heirs with Christ. They will have true security, which the loving God will not remove from those who love him. Human beings will rejoice to have all these things, as they will if someone else they love has them. Indeed, in perfect charity, all will rejoice as much for others as for themselves. And, just as everyone will love God more than himself, so everyone will rejoice more in God's happiness than in his own. They will love God so much that their hearts, minds and souls will be too small for the greatness and fullness of their love and joy.

Chapter XXVI (pp. 24–5)

Anselm asks if this is the joy that God has announced through his Son. Even when human beings are full of joy, there will still be more joy to come. In this life, they have not seen or heard how much they will love and know God in their future life.

Anselm prays to God that he will know and love God, in order to rejoice in him. Through Jesus, God has counselled human beings to ask, and has promised that they will receive. He asks to receive, so that his joy may be full. In the meantime, he wants to think, and speak about, and love God and the future life, until he enters into the joy of God, the Three in One.

Overview of Gaunilo's **Reply on Behalf of the Fool** (*pp. 28–33*)

A being than which none greater can be thought

Gaunilo explains that, if someone doubts the existence of a being than which nothing greater can be thought, he is told that to be able to doubt its existence is to have it in the understanding, since the concept has been understood. And it must also exist in reality, because this is greater than existing only in the understanding. If it existed only in the understanding, that which is greater than everything else (as he puts it) would not be, involving a contradiction. So, what is greater than everything else must exist in reality, as well as in the understanding.

The understanding contains many false things

However, his understanding contains many false things. He understands them, but they do not actually exist. So, there is a need to establish that this being cannot be thought of in the same way as false or doubtful things, and that it cannot exist in the understanding without it being genuinely known that it actually exists.

Even God can be thought not to exist

But this would mean that there would be no distinction between having something in the understanding, and then later understanding that it exists, as with a painting, which first exists in the painter's mind and then in the completed picture. It also seems impossible to accept that this being cannot be thought not to exist, as even God can be. Proof is required that this being has only to be thought of for the understanding to see certainly that it exists. It is not enough to say that it exists in the understanding, because many false or doubtful things are understood.

That which is greater than everything else that can be thought is not like anything else

Gaunilo states that he is no more able to think of that which is greater than everything else that can be thought, in terms of anything he knows, than he can of God; but he can think of both as not existing. If he heard about a person he did not know, he could think of him in terms of men in general and, even if it turned out that the particular man did not exist, he would have thought of him on the basis of something real. However, when he is told about God, or something greater than everything else, he does not have it in his understanding in the same way, because there is nothing real, like men in general, on which to base his thinking. Such a being can only be thought about on the basis of the word itself; but the word's meaning and customary use are not known.

If it does not exist, everything that does exist will be greater than it

A further argument is that this thing, which has been proved to exist in the understanding, must actually exist; otherwise, everything that exists will be greater than it. Gaunilo does not deny that it exists in his understanding, even though it cannot be thought of on the basis of anything known. But its actual existence cannot be inferred from this. He also denies that it is greater than any real thing, or that it exists at all, except to the extent that existence can be ascribed to something that is completely unknown. The so-called proof that it is greater than everything else does not show it actually exists. And it exists in his understanding only as doubtful and uncertain things do.

The lost island

He refers to the story of a lost island, which is supposed to be a perfect place to live. The story can be understood, but somebody might then argue that, as it exists in the understanding, and existence in reality is better, it must exist in reality. If not, any land that does is greater. But for the argument to be convincing, it would need to exist in the understanding as something that truly and undoubtedly exists in reality.

The highest being cannot be thought not to exist

The next claim is that this being cannot fail to exist, even in thought; otherwise, it would not be greater than everything else. But Gaunilo demands proof that a superior being, greater and better than all others, does actually exist. Rather than saying that the highest being cannot be thought not to exist, it would be better to say that it cannot be understood not to exist. False things cannot be understood, although they can be thought. He certainly knows that he himself exists, but also that he can fail to exist, whereas God exists, and cannot fail to exist. He is not sure whether he could think he does not exist, while knowing certainly that he does. But if he could, this would be possible for anything else he certainly knows to exist. If not, it is not only God who cannot be thought not to exist.

The rest of the Proslogion is well argued

He acknowledges that the rest of the *Proslogion* is cogently argued; it should not be belittled because the opening chapters are not.

Overview of Anselm's **Reply to Gaunilo** *(pp. 36–46)*

His critic is not actually a fool

Anselm begins by acknowledging that Gaunilo is not a fool but a Christian.

God is that than which a greater cannot be thought

Gaunilo has said that something than which a greater cannot be thought is not in the understanding any differently from something that cannot be thought according to the true nature of anything at all; and that, just because it exists in the understanding, it does not follow that it actually exists. But, if it does not, God is not that than which a greater cannot be thought; and, if he is neither understood nor thought, he exists neither in the understanding nor in thought. Gaunilo's faith should tell him that this is not so, and that that than which a greater cannot be thought is understood and thought, and exists in the understanding and in thought.

If such a being can be thought to exist, or can be thought at all, it exists necessarily

Gaunilo maintains that it does not follow from the fact that the concept is understood that it exists in the understanding, and that actual existence does not follow from existence in the understanding. But if it can be thought to exist, it must necessarily exist, because it cannot be thought of as beginning to exist, whereas things that can be thought to exist, but in fact do not, can be. So, it cannot be thought to exist, but not actually do so. If it can be thought to exist, or can be thought at all, it exists necessarily. Even those who doubt such a being's existence do not doubt that, if it existed, it would not be able to fail to exist, either in reality or in the understanding. If it could, it would not be that than which a greater cannot be thought. But something that can be thought, but which does not actually exist, could.

It cannot be thought not to exist

Something that can be thought, but does not exist, would not, if it existed, be that than which a greater cannot be thought. So, if it can be thought at all, it exists. Further, something, including time and the universe, that does not exist everywhere and always, can be thought not to exist anywhere or at any time. But, if it exists, that than which a greater cannot be thought, cannot be thought not to exist. If it could, it would not be that than which a greater cannot be thought.

It cannot exist only in the understanding

Anselm asks whether such a being can be thought and understood, and can exist in thought or in the understanding. It might be said not to be fully understood, but if someone hears the words, that than which a greater cannot be thought, he understands them. It might be argued that it does not follow from its existing in the understanding that it is understood. However, if it is understood, it must exist in the understanding, because this is how things are understood. But, if it exists only in the understanding, it both is, and is not, that than which a greater cannot be thought. If it can be thought actually to exist, that is greater than existence in the understanding alone. Therefore, it follows that it cannot exist only in the understanding, because then it would be that than which a greater can be thought.

The lost island

Anselm dismisses the lost island argument. There is nothing to which the inference in Anselm's argument could be applied, except that than which a greater cannot be thought.

Everything, apart from that which exists in the highest degree, can be thought not to exist

It might be said that it cannot be understood not to exist. However, thought is more correct, because otherwise it might be argued that nothing that exists can be understood not to exist, because that would be false. But even if something that actually exists cannot be understood not to exist, everything, apart from that which exists in the highest degree, can be thought not to. People can imagine things that they can think of as existing, which do not, and vice-versa. But they cannot think of something as existing and not existing at the same time. They can think of things that they know to exist as not existing, but this is not so with that than which a greater cannot be thought. God alone cannot be thought not to exist.

It is not that which is greater than everything else

Anselm points out that Gaunilo has misrepresented his argument. He did not write that that which is greater than everything else exists in the understanding and, if it does, exists in reality as well, because otherwise it would not be greater than everything else. That which is greater than everything else is not the same as that than which nothing greater can be thought. While it is clear that that than which a greater cannot be thought exists, is not capable of not existing, and cannot be thought not to exist, this is not true of Gaunilo's formulation. It is not obvious that something that can be thought not to exist is not greater than everything else that exists, nor is it obvious that it is the same as that than which a greater cannot be thought. If somebody said that something exists, which is greater than everything else that exists, but which can be thought not to exist, and that something greater than it can be thought, it would obviously not be greater than everything else that exists. And it would not be that than which a greater cannot be thought. The problem was that Gaunilo's formulation required a further premise. Only, that than which a greater cannot be thought could not be understood as anything other than the one thing that is greater than everything else.

False and doubtful things

As for Gaunilo's point about false or doubtful things, he (Anselm) was merely attempting to show that that than which a greater cannot be thought exists, in some form, in the understanding, before going on to determine whether it exists only in the understanding, like a false thing, or also in reality, like a real thing. If false and doubtful things are understood, and exist in the understanding, there is no reason why the being he was discussing cannot. Gaunilo's arguments are not consistent. He claims to understand what people mean if they say false things, but also that, if what he hears is not held in thought like false things, he would not say that he thinks it, and has it in his thought, but that he understands it and has it in his understanding, as he cannot think it without understanding it: that is, knowing that it exists in reality.

However, it is not consistent to say, on the one hand, that false things are understood in some sense, and, on the other, that to understand is to know that something exists. If it is possible to understand false things in some way, he should not criticize Anselm for saying that that than which a greater cannot be thought was understood and existed in the understanding, even before it was certain that it existed in reality.

That than which a greater cannot be thought is at least partly understood

Gaunilo's next point was about the difficulty of accepting that that than which a greater cannot be thought cannot be thought not to exist in the way that even God can be thought not to exist. But it does not make sense to deny the existence of something that is understood, because it is said to be the same as something whose existence is denied, because it is not understood. Nobody would deny the existence of that than which a greater cannot be thought because he denies God's existence. If, through lack of complete understanding, somebody does deny the existence of that than which a greater cannot be thought, it would be more straightforward to prove the existence of something that is partly understood than of something that is not understood at all. It is more sensible to speak of that than which a greater cannot be thought, which can be understood, than of God, which might not be.

The painter and the picture

Gaunilo claims that than which a greater cannot be thought is not like a yet-to-be-painted picture, which exists in the painter's understanding. But he is missing the point. He (Anselm) had not introduced this example, because it is the same sort of thing as that than which a greater cannot be thought, but to show that something can exist in the understanding, which is understood not to exist in reality.

Inferences from lesser to greater goods

Gaunilo contends that he cannot think of that than which a greater cannot be thought as related to anything he knows. However, lesser goods, by being good, resemble greater ones, so inferences about that than which a greater cannot be thought can be made from things that are not. Orthodox Christians who think otherwise should remember Romans 1.20, which states that God's everlasting power and divinity are clearly seen through the things he has made.

The expression, that than which a greater cannot be thought, can be thought and understood

Even if that than which a greater cannot be thought cannot be thought or understood, it is not wrong to say that the expression itself can be. A thing can be said to be unthinkable, although it cannot be thought. Similarly, the expression, that than which a greater cannot be thought, can be thought and understood, even though the thing itself cannot be: anybody who denies its existence is thinking and understanding what he denies. It is also possible to think and understand something that cannot fail to exist, and anybody thinking of that than which a greater cannot be thought is thinking of something that cannot fail to exist; and so of something that exists necessarily.

Gaunilo's criticisms were made in a friendly spirit

Despite Gaunilo's criticisms, Anselm considers his proof of God's existence to be fairly conclusive. When that than which a greater cannot be thought is thought or understood, it is necessarily proved to exist in reality. However, he is grateful to Gaunilo for both his praise and his criticism. He had praised what he agreed with, and made his criticisms in a friendly spirit.

Glossary

Adam. The story of Adam (and Eve) is told in Genesis, the first book of the Old Testament. Although enjoying a perfect relationship with God, Adam, the first man, chose to disobey God. Anselm bemoans the fact that, through his disobedience, Adam brought (original) sin and death into the world, and put human beings at a distance from God. See original sin below.

Ages of time. God is eternal, and so transcends time. Anselm emphasizes how different God is from human beings by saying that his eternity contains all the ages of time.

Analogy. Drawing a parallel between two things on the basis of similarities between them.

Angels. Heavenly beings who, in the Christian tradition, are well-disposed towards human beings and act as God's messengers to them.

A posteriori. That which comes after, or is based on, experience/empirical evidence.

A priori. That which comes before experience, and which holds (or is claimed to hold) irrespective of experience.

Aquinas, Saint Thomas (c. 1225–74). Italian-born philosopher and theologian and Dominican friar. Aquinas rejects the ontological argument in his *Summa Theologica*, preferring proofs of God's existence that start from his effects (the world) to one that starts from the concept of God. Aquinas' rejection of the argument meant that little attention was given to it, until Descartes revived interest in it in the seventeenth century.

Beauty. Anselm emphasizes God's spiritual beauty by referring to him in physical terms, such as harmony, fragrance and softness. He regrets the fact that, as God is hidden from his soul, he cannot see his beauty.

Beneficial. Advantageous. Because they are not beneficial, Anselm describes such powers as the ability to lie as weaknesses.

Body. God does not have a body, so Anselm wonders how, without senses, God can see. He concludes that, as God knows everything (is omniscient), he can be said to see everything.

Bounded. Limited.

Canonization. Recognition by the Roman Catholic Church of a person as a saint.

Cease, or begin, to exist. As God is eternal, unlike created beings, he did not begin to exist, nor will he cease to exist.

Changeable. Created things change: they come into existence and they cease to exist. But God is unchanging, or immutable.

Christian. Follower of Christianity. In Anselm's time, a member of the (Roman) Catholic Church.

Co-exist. Exist together, alongside each other. Anselm wonders how God's justice and mercy can co-exist.

Comfort. Consolation. As God is merciful, he is a source of comfort to the sorrowful.

Compassion. (Feeling of) pity or sympathy, which leads someone to help others. As God is impassible (does not experience emotion), he does not actually feel compassion for human beings. However, because he is merciful, he spares sinners, who feel the effects of his mercy.

Concept. Idea/understanding of a term, and being able to use it accurately.

Concord. Harmony, agreement.

Conjecture. Opinion that is not adequately supported by evidence.

Contemplation. A kind of prayer, which involves focusing intensely on God.

Contradiction. Bringing together a proposition and its negation. Anselm argues that, if that than which a greater cannot be thought, can be thought not to exist, it is not that than which a greater cannot be thought, which would be a contradiction.

Cosmological argument. One of the traditional arguments for the existence of God, which argues from the existence of the world and/or how it exists to God as its cause. In his *Summa Theologica*, Thomas Aquinas argues (second way or proof of the existence of God) that, as everything has a cause, there must either be an infinite regress of causes or a first cause, and, as there cannot be an infinite regress of causes, there must be a first cause of the world, God; and (third way or proof of the existence of God): the world consists of things that could not-exist (or 'contingent' things); but, if only such things existed, there must have been a time when nothing existed, in which case nothing would exist now; therefore, there must exist a being that cannot not-exist (a being that exists necessarily).

Created spirit. A spirit, such as an angel, who has been created (made) by God.

Created things. Things that have been created by God. Anselm contrasts the earthly delight human beings have in created things with the kind of intense delight they will find in God, their creator.

Creator. Term applied to God as the maker of the universe. In Christian theology, God made the universe from nothing.

Darkness. Anselm contrasts the darkness of the lives human beings lead, following the sin of Adam, with the light of God, from which they have been shut out.

Descartes, René (1596–1650). French philosopher and mathematician. In his *Meditations on First Philosophy* (Meditation V), Descartes puts forward a version of the ontological argument for God's existence.

Design argument. One of the traditional arguments for the existence of God, which points to similarities between the world and objects designed and made by human beings, and argues that, as the effects are similar, the causes must also be similar.

Effect. What results from something, its consequences. Human beings feel the effects of God's mercy, in that he spares rather than punishes them.

Emotion. Feeling: which God does not experience, as he is impassible.

Eternal/eternity. In the Christian context, the idea that God transcends time. God has no past or future, but is always present everywhere.

Eternal death. Being shut out from God, through being condemned to hell, as (Anselm feels) the wicked deserve.

Everlasting life. Living forever with God in heaven.

Everywhere at once. The idea that God is omnipresent.

Evil and guilty creatures. Human beings, who have inherited original sin, as a result of the fall, who continue to disobey God, and who do not deserve God's goodness.

Exists 'necessarily'. See necessary existence below.

Eye of my soul. Anselm pictures the soul as having an eye, which, as it seeks God, is blinded by God's supreme and inaccessible light.

Faith. In a religious context, this can be simply religious belief/belief in God, or trusting belief in God (his existence and/or his goodness), which is not supported by clear evidence. Anselm accepts that belief in God will not come from trying to understand God intellectually, but that to understand God, and that he exists, fully, it is first necessary to believe in him. However, he also believes that belief in God, and beliefs about God's nature, can have a rational basis, and are not just a matter of blind faith, from which reason is excluded. Hence, the *Proslogion* is, 'Faith seeking understanding'.

Fall (the). Human beings' choosing to disobey God, and the consequences: the ending of their perfect relationship with God and sin, and death entering the world. See also Adam above.

Father. Way of addressing, and thinking about the Christian God, which emphasizes his goodness and care for human beings, as in the opening words of the Lord's prayer.

Fool. Both Psalm 14 and Psalm 53 begin with the words, 'The fool says in his heart, "There is no God"'. The original Hebrew word does not suggest lack of intellectual ability, but rash dismissal of the truth about God.

Fragrance. Literally sweet smell. See beauty above.

Gaunilo. Eleventh-century monk from the Abbey of Marmoutier (Tours) who, in his *Reply on Behalf of the Fool* (the only writing of his that is known), challenged the argument for God's existence put forward by Anselm in the *Proslogion*.

Genus. Class of things, which have common characteristics, but which can be divided into different species.

God. In the *Proslogion*, the Christian God.

Grace. The help God freely gives to human beings through Jesus Christ.

Greater. Anselm's argument for God's existence starts with the idea that he is something than which nothing greater can be thought. See Context for discussion of the problems of Anselm's argument.

Harmony. Literally, a melodious sound. See beauty above.

Highest good. God, through whom everything that is good exists.

Highest spirit. God

Highest thing. God

Holy Spirit. In Christianity, the third person of the Trinity, who reveals God to human beings, and who inspires and strengthens Christians.

Hugo, Archbishop of Lyons. Apostolic legate in France, who encouraged Anselm to publish the *Proslogion* and the *Monologion*.

Image. According to Christian teaching, human beings are made in the image or likeness of God. (See Genesis 1.27.) However, as a result of their disobedience, and their consequent sinfulness, this likeness was damaged.

Immortality. Not dying, living on forever (and in Christian teaching) in a perfect relationship with God. Human beings had originally been immortal, but their disobedience brought death into the world. (See Genesis 3.19.)

Impassible. Incapable of emotion. Anselm discusses this attribute of God at length in *Proslogion*, Chapter VIII.

Inaccessible. That which cannot be reached, or which is not open. In *Proslogion*, Chapter XVI, Anselm refers to the eye of his soul being dazzled by God's inaccessible light.

Incomprehensible. That which cannot be understood, as God's goodness cannot be by human beings.

Inconsistency. When two things, ideas, actions are incompatible/at odds with each other.

Ineffable. That which cannot be expressed or uttered.

Inference/infer. Concluding one thing from something else. In his *Reply to Gaunilo*, Anselm argues that the inference in his argument in *Proslogion*, Chapters II–IV can only be applied to that than which a greater cannot be thought/ God.

Intellect. Mind, faculty of knowing and understanding.

Jesus Christ (c. BC 5/6–c. 30 AD). Founder of Christianity, who is the incarnate Word of God and second person of the Trinity.

Joint-heirs with Christ. In Romans 8.17, Paul explains that Christians are 'joint-heirs with Christ': they share his sufferings in order that they may also share his glory.

Just/justice. Treating people fairly, people being treated fairly or receiving their due. In *Proslogion*, Chapters IX and X, Anselm discusses the apparent conflict between God's justice and mercy: he spares the wicked, even though they deserve to be condemned to eternal death.

Kant, Immanuel (1724–1804). Influential German philosopher, whose writings cover metaphysics, moral philosophy and philosophy of religion. In his *Critique of Pure Reason*, Kant refutes the ontological argument, although his criticisms are directed specifically at Descartes' version, rather than Anselm's. (See Context.)

Law of place/law of time. Unlike human beings, God is not subject to laws of place and time. He is unbounded, and can be wholly everywhere at once.

Lie. Say what is untrue. In *Proslogion*, Chapter VII, Anselm argues that the ability to lie shows weakness, not power, as it means that wickedness has power over the liar.

Light. God dwells in dazzling light, which is inaccessible to human beings as a result of their disobedience and sin. God's light is identified with truth, from which comes every truth which enlightens the rational mind, and in which is everything that is true (*Proslogion*, Chapters XIV and XVI).

Lost Island. In his *Reply on Behalf of the Fool*, Gaunilo maintains that Anselm's argument in *Proslogion*, Chapters II–IV could be used to prove the existence of a mythical Lost Island, because it could be claimed that, if it is the most excellent human habitation, and it is more excellent to exist in reality than only in the understanding, it must exist in reality.

Love. In Christian theology, God is all-loving, and, despite their sinfulness, loves human beings so much that he sent his son, Jesus Christ, to redeem them.

Made all other things from nothing. In Christian theology, God created the universe and everything it contains from nothing, so it is wholly dependent on him for its existence and continuation.

Material object. A physical object, bodily being. In *Proslogion*, Chapter XIII, Anselm compares and contrasts God, created spirits and material objects. Material objects are completely bounded; created spirits can be wholly in more than one place, but not everywhere; only God can be wholly everywhere at once.

Meditation. Deep, sustained and reverent reflection on God or religious idea.

Merciful. Having or showing mercy. God (*Proslogion*, Chapter VIII) shows his mercy to human beings by sparing sinners, but, because he is impassible, does not experience any feeling of compassion. See also just/justice above.

Merits. In the *Proslogion*, deserts rather than deserving well. The just are saved with the help of their merits, sinners despite their merits (Chapter IX).

Monologion. Anselm's first book, 'A pattern for meditation on the rational basis of faith'. Anselm explains, in the Prologue to the *Proslogion*, that he was dissatisfied with the *Monologion*, because it consisted of a 'chaining together' of arguments for God's existence, rather than the 'single argument' that he puts forward in the *Proslogion* (Chapters II–IV).

Mortal. Subject to death. Human beings became subject to death as a result of the fall.

Necessary existence. The kind of existence Anselm claims that than which a greater cannot be thought has. Such a being must exist in reality, because to exist in reality is greater than existing only in the understanding, so, if it does not exist, it is not that than which nothing greater can be thought, because a greater being (one that exists in reality) can be thought. Further, a being which cannot be thought of as not-existing is greater than a being which can be thought of as not-existing. But if the being than which a greater cannot be thought can be thought of as not-existing, that being is not that than which a greater cannot be thought. And this is a contradiction.

Non-existence. Apart from God, everything that exists comes into existence out of non-existence, and so is changeable; returns to non-existence; and can be thought of as not existing (*Proslogion*, Chapter XXII).

Omnipotent. In Christian teaching, God's power is unlimited, so he is omnipotent.

Ontological argument. One of the traditional arguments for the existence of God, which argues from the concept of God to his existence, as Anselm does in the *Proslogion*. The argument was rejected by Aquinas in the *Summa Theologica*, but revived by Descartes in his *Meditations on First Philosophy*. Kant provides a detailed refutation of the ontological argument (together with the other traditional arguments for God's existence) in his *Critique of Pure Reason*. See necessary existence above and Context.

Original sin. The teaching that human nature was damaged by the fall, and that human beings inherit an inclination to sin.

Orthodox Christian. Christian who accepts his Church's (in this case the Roman Catholic Church) teachings, and does not challenge them.

Outside time altogether. God's eternity means that he is

71

outside time, Anselm discusses the implications of this in *Proslogion*, Chapter XIX.

Part. Unlike created things, God does not consist of parts. He is unity itself, and cannot be broken up either in fact or understanding (*Proslogion*, Chapter XVIII).

Percipient. Far-seeing, seeing things clearly, seeing things which cannot be discerned by the senses.

Perfect charity. As joint-heirs of Christ and sharers in his glory, God's faithful servants will, in the life to come, exist in a state of perfect mutual love, in which they will love God more than themselves and rejoice for each other (*Proslogion*, Chapters XXV and XXVI).

Premise. One of the propositions in an argument, on the basis of which the conclusion is reached.

Proceeds. In the *Proslogion*, come forth from. The Holy Spirit proceeds from Father and Son (God and Christ). See Holy Spirit above and Trinity below.

Proslogion. Anselm's second book, 'Faith seeking understanding', in which (as he claims at the end of the *Reply to Gaunilo*), he considered that he had provided 'a quite conclusive proof' of God's existence.

Prove God's existence. Both the *Monologion* and the *Proslogion* were attempts to prove God's existence, although, in the *Proslogion* (Chapter I), Anselm acknowledges that belief precedes understanding, suggesting that, to understand his proof, it is first necessary to believe in God.

Rational basis of faith. See faith above.

Rational mind. A mind willing to be guided by reason.

Retribution. Deserved punishment for wrong(s) committed.

Righteous. Upright, virtuous.

Salvation. In Christianity, God intervening, through Jesus, to save/redeem human beings, despite their disobedience and sin, and give them eternal life with him.

Save(d). See salvation above.

Savour. See beauty above.

Self-sufficient. God is self-sufficient: he has not been created by, nor does his continued existence depend upon, anything else.

Senses. Human beings gain knowledge through their senses, but God does not require senses, because he is omniscient/all-knowing.

Sin. Offence against, disobedience of, God.

Softness. See beauty above.

Son. See Trinity below.

Sons of God. According to Matthew 5.9, those who are peacemakers (create peace in the world) will be called sons of God.

Sorrowful. Those who grieve because of evil/sin.

Soul. In Christianity, the spiritual element within human beings, which is the seat of personality and individual identity, which lives on after death, and which will be reunited with its body at the general resurrection.

Spatial extension. Occupy space, have a body.

Species. The sub-groups into which a genus is divided.

Spirit. Non-physical being, such as an angel.

Substance. The essence of something, which makes it what it is.

Supreme nature. God. Gaunilo does not accept that the idea of the supreme nature/God exists in the understanding, because there is nothing equivalent to it in our experience, to enable us to understand what it means.

Supremely good. God is all-good or omnibenevolent.

Supremely just. As God is supremely just, he spares sinners, who deserve eternal death.

Three in One. See Trinity below.

Time and the universe. Unlike God, the whole of time does not always exist, and the whole universe is not everywhere.

Trinity. In Christianity, God exists in three, co-equal persons:

Father, Son and Holy Spirit. However, this does not mean that God is divided into three or that there are three Gods. God's unity is preserved, because the three persons are of one substance (one being) and so God is three in one. The teaching has been a subject of debate and (intense) disagreement over the centuries. It is helpful to think in terms of three modes of existence: God the Father: the creator; God the Son, Jesus: the redeemer; and the Holy Spirit: the inspirer and sustainer of Christians and the Christian Church.

True security. Those who believe in, and obey, God will have true security because, as joint-heirs with Christ, they will share his glory.

Unbounded. Without limit.

Understanding. See prove God's existence above.

Unity itself. God is One. He does not consist of parts.

Vastness. This is a reference, not to God's physical size (he does not have a body), but to his overwhelming superiority to human beings. Anselm is aware of how far God is from his sight; yet, he is always present in God's (*Proslogion*, Chapter XVI).

Vision of God. As a result of the fall, human beings had gone from living in God's presence and being immortal to being at a distance from him and mortality.

Who alone exists through himself. God alone does not depend on anything else for his existence; he is not caused by anything else.

Wholly present. God is always present, or omnipresent.

Wicked. Sinful, immoral, vicious.

Word. Jesus Christ, who is God's Word, through whom he expresses himself and communicates with human beings.